W0323456

Fun and Practice 2

Materialien zur Freiarbeit für die Klasse 6

Lösungsheft

von
Gerd Hesterberg
Brigitte Seidl
Jochen Vatter

Ernst Klett Verlag
Stuttgart München Düsseldorf Leipzig

CONTENTS

Teacher's Notes

In diesem Heft befinden sich die Lösungen zu den Kopiervorlagen aus dem Heft *Fun and Practice 2* (Klett-Nr. 506940). Ein wichtiges Merkmal von *Fun and Practice 2* ist die Möglichkeit zum selbständigen Arbeiten und zur Kontrolle durch die Schülerinnen und Schüler selbst in sogenannter Freiarbeit. Um dem Sinn und Zweck von Freiarbeit gerecht zu werden, sollen diese Lösungen leicht zugänglich sein, damit Schülerinnen und Schüler diese schnell einsehen können, um die Selbstkontrolle zu ermöglichen. Es bietet sich an, die Lösungen in doppelter Anzahl in Klarsichthüllen in einem Ordner zur Verfügung zu stellen. Somit können mehrere Schüler und Schülerinnen gleichzeitig bereits bearbeitete Arbeitsblätter kontrollieren. Zu den Spielvorlagen aus dem Arbeitsheft sowie zu den Kopiervorlagen 69 und 70 gibt es keine Lösungen. Bei folgenden Kopiervorlagen dient jeweils die Kopiervorlage in Originalform (aus dem Arbeitsheft) als Lösung – es erscheinen deshalb in diesem Lösungsheft keine Lösungen dazu: Kopiervorlagen 2, 20, 21, 25, 39, 40, 59, 66 und 68. Zu manchen Aufgaben sind mehrere Lösungen möglich, so daß es nicht möglich ist, eine Musterlösung zu bieten. In solchen Fällen werden Schülerinnen und Schüler aufgefordert, ihre eigenen Lösungen dem Lehrer bzw. der Lehrerin zur Kontrolle zu zeigen. Überhaupt sollte man Schülerinnen und Schülern klarmachen, daß die Lösungen als Musterlösungen zu betrachten sind, und daß sie sich bei eventuellen Abweichungen bei ihrer Lehrperson melden sollen.

The Breakfast Table

1. What can you see on the breakfast table? Write the names of the things.
(Schreibe die Namen der Dinge, die du auf dem Tisch siehst.)

2. Write down what you can see on the table.

There is some butter, a tea pot, a bottle of milk, some toast, some cornflakes and some sugar.

There are two plates, two cups, two saucers, two knives, two forks and two tea spoons.

3. Now colour the things in.
The plates are blue and white. The tea pot is red. The knives, forks and spoons are black. The cups are green, the saucers are green and white. The butter is yellow. The bread is brown. The bottle of milk is white. And the cornflakes are red and brown.

[4.] Draw your own breakfast table and write the names of the things on it.

• • • • • • • • • • • • • • • • **FOLD HERE** • • • • • • • • • • • • • • • •

Here are the names of the things on the table:

fork plate knife tea spoon sugar bottle of milk
tea pot bread/toast butter cup saucer cornflakes

9

A piece of cake

1. Write the words under the right pictures.

piece	bag	packet	glass	**of**	eggs	milk	toast	beans	coke
tin	bottle	cup	box		coffee	crisps	tea	biscuits

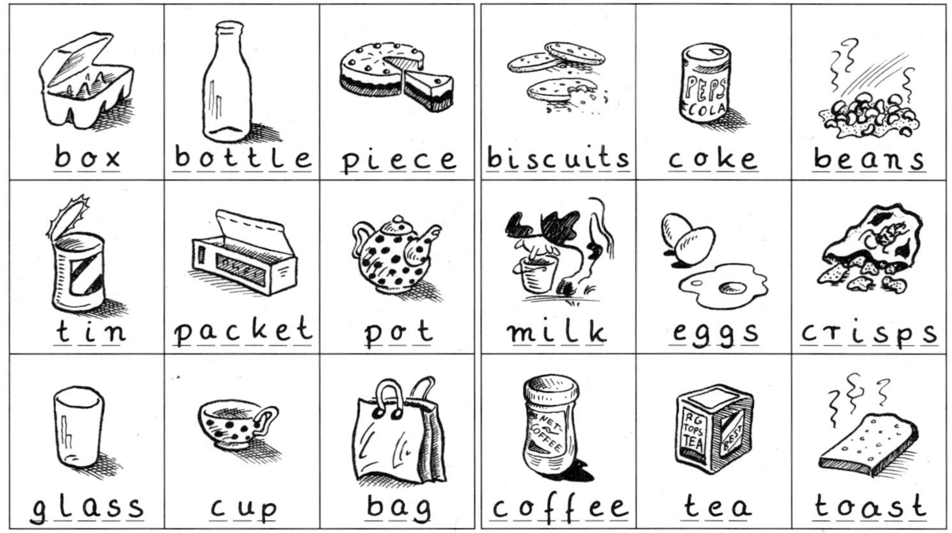

box	bottle	piece	biscuits	coke	beans
tin	packet	pot	milk	eggs	crisps
glass	cup	bag	coffee	tea	toast

2. What goes together?

A box of eggs.
A bottle of milk.
A piece of toast.
A tin of beans.
A cup of coffee.
A packet of biscuits.
A pot of tea.
A glass of milk.
A bag of crisps.

What does Robin want? What doesn't he want?

He wants a bag of potatoes. He doesn't want a pot of tea.
He wants a packet of biscuits.
He doesn't want a box of eggs.
He wants a tin of coke.
He doesn't want a cup of coffee.
He wants a bag of crisps.
He doesn't want a bottle of milk.
He wants a piece of bread.
He doesn't want a tin of beans.

11

Breakfast in Bed

There is one word wrong in each sentence. Correct the sentences.
(Korrigiere die Sätze und schreibe sie richtig hin.)

1. It is Mr King's birthday. It is Mrs King's birthday.
2. Mrs King is very thirsty. Mrs King is very hungry.
3. The dog's name is Dandy. The dog's name is Goofy.
4. Mr King drops the breakfast on the floor. Mr King drops the breakfast on the bed.
5. Goofy is a very clever dog. Goofy is a very silly dog.

Mrs Do-Does and Mr Don't-Doesn't

Here are two funny characters:
Mrs Do-Does and Mr Don't-Doesn't.
Mrs Do-Does is a reporter.
Mr Don't-Doesn't comes from Jupiter.
Mrs Do-Does asks Mr Don't-Doesn't a lot of questions.

1. Can you complete the questions and answers?
(Kannst du die Fragen und Antworten der beiden vervollständigen?)

Do or Does?	don't or doesn't?
Do you live in a house?	No, I don't. I live outside.
Does your mother speak English?	No, she doesn't. She speaks 'Jupitan'.
Does your father watch TV?	No, he doesn't. We haven't got a TV.
Does your sister play tennis?	No, she doesn't. She plays robot-roller.
Do you go shopping on Jupiter?	No, I don't. There aren't any shops on Jupiter!
Do you and your parents have tea for breakfast?	No, we don't. We have 10 litres of water for breakfast.
Does your brother go to school?	No, he doesn't. There aren't any schools on Jupiter.
Do you sleep in a bed?	No, I don't. I sleep in a space-bag.
Does your father read many books?	No, he doesn't. He can't read!
I like jam tarts. Do you like jam tarts, too?	No, I don't. They are too sweet.

[2.] Now Mrs Do-Does asks you the questions. Write your answers in your exercise book.

Do Does Don't Doesn't

Setze die Flugblätter aus dem Flugzeug richtig in die Fragen und Anworten unten ein.

Do ___ you live in a caravan? No, I don't.
Does ___ your mother speak English? No, she doesn't.
Does ___ your father watch TV every day? No, he doesn't.
Does ___ Mary play tennis? Yes, she does.
Do ___ you go shopping on Saturdays? Yes, I do.
Do ___ your parents drink tea for breakfast? No, they don't.
Does ___ Peter's brother go to school? Yes, he does.
Do ___ you sleep in the living room? No, I don't.
Does ___ Christopher read many books? Yes, he does.
Do ___ you like jam tarts? No, I don't.
Does ___ Louise read comics? Yes, she does.
Does ___ Alan like potatoes? No, he doesn't.
Do ___ your pets watch TV? No, they don't.
Do ___ you speak English? Yes, I do.
Does ___ Fred speak French? No, he doesn't.
Do ___ Henry and Fred like fish and chips? Yes, they do.
Do ___ Simon and Helen work in a supermarket? No, they don't.
Does ___ David want a hamburger? No, he doesn't.

Eines der Flugblätter wird nicht eingesetzt. Darauf steht: doesn't

WORD GAMES

At the shops

Write the English words.

Who works in a shop? ↓ shop assistant

Regalbrett	shelf
nichts	nothing
Schaufenster	shop window
Pfund	pound
wünschen	want
schließen	close
verkaufen	sell
sonst noch etwas	anything else
Supermarkt	supermarket
nehmen	take
Korb	basket
öffnen	open
Dose	tin

In a pet shop

Write the English words.

1	FISH
2	HAMSTER
3	SHELF
4	MOUSE
5	GUINEA PIG
6	BUDGIE
7	RABBIT
8	TORTOISE
9	TANK
10	PARROT
11	DOG
12	CAGE

One fish, two fish

1. Find the fish in the tank. Colour them in.

2. How many fish are there?

There are *six* fish in the tank.

3. Can you remember the plurals of these words?

one fish	two fish
one man	two men
one woman	two *women*
one child	two *children*
one sheep	two *sheep*
one mouse	two *mice*
one knife	two *knives*
one shelf	two *shelves*

4. Can you find the words and join them together?

A CROSSWORD PUZZLE

Across →

4 ~~Samstag~~
7 alle
8 draußen
10 spanisch
13 
15 französisch
16 
17 das, jenes
19 italienisch
21 
22 gehen, fahren
23 
25 
28 Zug
31 warten
32 sitzen
33 Sommer
34 
35 
36 

Down ↓

1 
2 halten
3 anhalten
5 oberes Ende
6 laufen
9 Abend
10 
11 immer
12 Jahreszeit
14 wieder
15 Familie
18 
20 
21 rufen
24 Herbst
26 bellen
27 richtig, echt
29 Regen, regnen
30 in, hinein
32 sehen

Put in the English words.

There's work to do!

1. Look at the pictures and then complete the sentences. The words in the box will help you. *(Schaue die Bilder an, dann vervollständige die Sätze. Die Wörter in dem Kästchen werden dir helfen.)*

bus driver	shop	teacher	shop assistant	farmer	factory	office
office worker	garage	factory worker	farm	clown	bus	circus

Buster works on a bus. He's a bus driver.
Carol works at a garage. She's a car mechanic.
Fiona works at a factory. She's a factory worker.
Terry works at a school. He's a teacher.
Clarence works in a circus. He's a clown.
Sheila works in a shop. She's a shop assistant.
Oliver works in an office. He's an office worker.
Fred works on a farm. He's a farmer.

2. Fred and Oliver talk about their jobs. Who says what?

- I sometimes drive a tractor.
- I often work in the fields.
- I use the telephone a lot.
- I get up at seven.
- I get up at five.
- I work in an office.
- In summer I often finish work at 7.00 or 8.00 in the evening.
- I start work at 5.30.
- I always finish work at 5.00 pm.
- I write a lot.
- I start work at 8.00.

Fred: *I get up at* five.
I start work at 5.30.
I often work in the fields.
I sometimes drive a tractor.
In summer I often finish work at 7.00 or 8.00 in the evening.

Oliver: *I get up at* seven.
I start work at 8.00.
I use the telephone a lot.
I work in an office.
I write a lot.
I always finish work at 5.00 pm.

John's new job

John is talking to Mrs Bailey. Mrs Bailey has got a book shop. John is the new shop assistant.

On Friday evening John telephones his friend Paula. She asks him about his day at work.

1. Complete John's answers. *(Vervollständige Johns Antworten.)*

Where do you work? *In Mrs Bailey's bookshop.*

What time do you start work?
At nine.

What do you do in the mornings? *I* clean the bookshelves. Then I put new books on the shelves.

When do you go for lunch? At one o'clock.

When does the shop open in the afternoon? At two o'clock.

What do you do in the afternoons? I help Mrs Bailey sell the books.

When do you go home in the evening? At half past six.

[2.] Write about John's day.

John starts work at nine. *In the morning he* cleans the bookshelves. Then he puts new books on the shelves. At one o'clock he goes for lunch. He has to be back at two o'clock. In the afternoon he helps Mrs Bailey sell the books. He goes home at half past six.

[3] Practise the telephone conversation with your partner. Then ask your partner some questions about John's day.

Example: Where does John work?
When does . . . ?

Countries and Languages

Mr and Mrs Hines are planning their summer holiday. They don't know where to go. And they can't speak many languages!
(Mr und Mrs Hines planen ihren nächsten Urlaub. Sie wissen nicht, wohin sie reisen sollen. Und sie sprechen leider nicht sehr viele Fremdsprachen!)

1. Look at the map and complete what they are saying.
(Schau die Karte an und vervollständige ihr Gespräch.)

Mr Hines: Let's go to (1) Turkey.

Mrs Hines: Oh no, I don't speak Turkish. How about (2) Greece?

Mr Hines: Oh no! I don't speak Greek. But (3) Italy is a nice country.

Mrs Hines: Oh no! I don't speak Italian

Can't we go to (4) Austria?

Mr Hines: Oh no! I don't speak German.

But perhaps you'd like to go to (5) Spain?

Mrs Hines: Oh no! I don't speak Spanish

Mr Hines: Well, let's stay at home then.

Mrs Hines: Oh no! Let's go to (6) France. We can speak French.

2. Charly is one of the clowns at a circus. One day a letter comes for him. It's from Greece. But Charly can only speak English, so he can't read the letter. He asks the other people at the circus to help him.

Jean: I'm from Paris. I'm French.

Pedro: I'm from Madrid. I'm Spanish.

Tahsin: I'm from Ankara. I'm Turkish.

Leonidas: I'm from Athens. I'm Greek.

Jochen: I'm from Berlin. I'm German.

Who can help Charly read the letter? Leonidas.

FOLD HERE

Here are the countries and the languages:

TURKEY FRANCE ITALY GREECE SPANISH FRENCH
AUSTRIA SPAIN GREEK ITALIAN TURKISH GERMAN

Tanja and Tom

Tanja, a 19-year-old German girl, is visiting her aunt and uncle in England.
At a cafeteria she has a talk with Tom, an English boy. He is asking Tanja some questions.

Er möchte wissen	*Sie antwortet*
– *aus welchem Land sie kommt*	*aus Deutschland*
– *ob sie in einer großen Stadt wohnt*	*nein, in einer kleinen Stadt*
– *ob deutsche Schüler und Schülerinnen Englisch in der Schule lernen*	*ja*
– *ob Tanja zur Schule geht*	*nein*
– *welchen Beruf sie hat*	*Kraftfahrzeugmechanikerin*
– *wo sie arbeitet*	*in einer Autowerkstatt*
– *ob viele Mädchen in der Werkstatt arbeiten*	*nein, nur zwei*
– *ob sie mit dem Auto zur Arbeit fährt*	*nein, mit dem Bus*
– *wann sie morgens mit der Arbeit beginnt*	*um 7.30 Uhr*
– *wann die Arbeit endet*	*um 16.30 Uhr*
– *wo sie zu Mittag ißt*	*in der Autowerkstatt*
– *was sie zu Mittag ißt*	*einige belegte Brote*
– *ob sie auch samstags arbeitet*	*nein*

These are Tom's questions. Can you make up the dialogue?

What's your job? Do you go to school? Do German pupils learn English at school? What do you have for lunch? Where do you have lunch? Do you work on Saturdays? Do you go to work by car? When do you start work in the morning? When do you finish work? Do you live in a big town? What country do you come from? Where do you work? Do many girls work at the garage?

Tom:	Tanja:
What country do you come from?	Germany.
Do you live in a big town?	No, in a small town.
Do German pupils learn English at school?	Yes, they do.
Do you go to school?	No, I don't.
What's your job?	I'm a car mechanic.
Where do you work?	At a garage.
Do many girls work at the garage?	No, only two.
Do you go to work by car?	No, by bus.
When do you start work in the morning?	At 7.30.
When do you finish work?	At half past four.
Where do you have lunch?	At the garage.
What do you have for lunch?	Some sandwiches.
Do you work on Saturdays?	No, I don't.

FOLD HERE

Here are Tanja's answers:
No, I don't. / At a garage. / Germany. / Yes, they do. / I'm a car mechanic. / At 7.30. / No, in a small town.
No, by bus. / At half past four. / At the garage. / Some sandwiches / No, only two.

Nice people – Nice clothes

1. Write the names of the clothes.

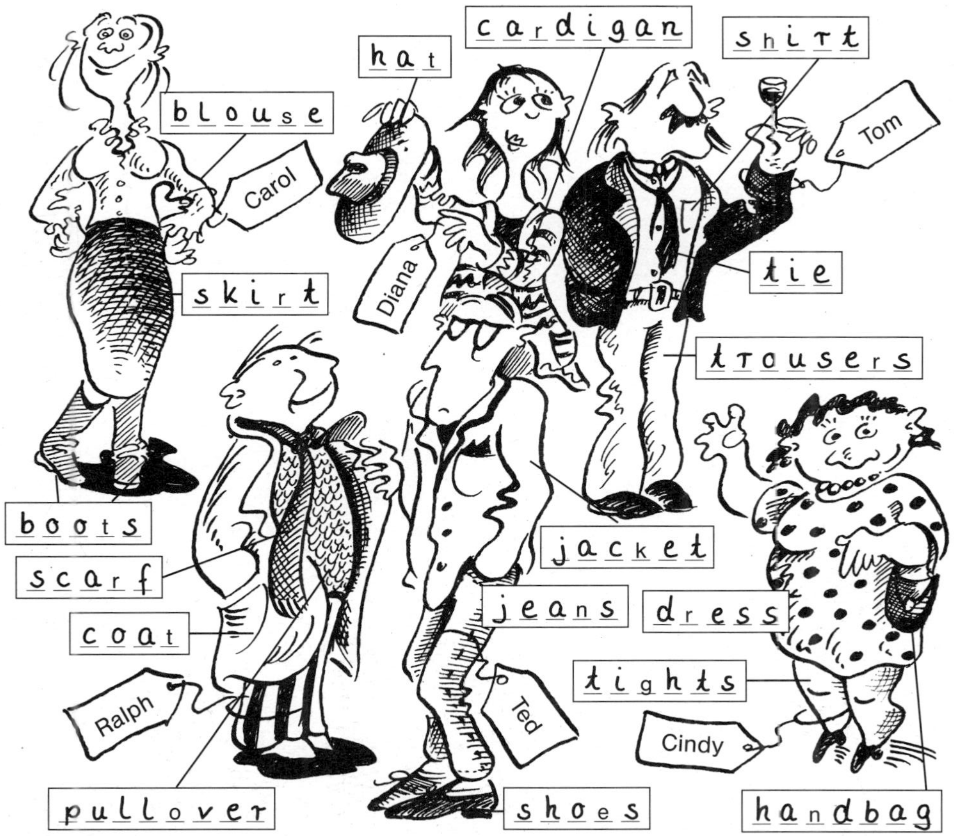

2. Who is it?

He/She is wearing a coat. That's Ralph.

She is wearing a skirt. That's Carol.

She is wearing a long cardigan. That's Diana.

He/She is wearing jeans and a jacket. That's Ted.

He/She is wearing a shirt and a tie. That's Tom.

He/She is wearing boots. That's Carol.

She is wearing a dress. That's Cindy.

He/She is wearing a pullover. That's Ralph.

3. Now write about the people in your exercise book.

Carol is wearing a blouse, boots *and a* skirt. Diana is...

• • • • • • • • • • • • • • • • • **FOLD HERE** • • • • • • • • • • • • • • • • • •

This will help you: COATCARDIGANHATDRESSTROUSERSSCARFTIGHTSSHOESBOOTS TIEJEANSHANDBAGSKIRTSHIRTBLOUSEJACKETPULLOVER

Bigger and Smaller

1. Who is it?

He is bigger than Alf, but smaller than Mickey. That's Tim.

He is smaller than Susan and Pam. That's Alf.

She is bigger than Susan, but smaller than Tim. That's Pam.

She is the biggest girl. That's Pam.

He is the smallest boy. That's Alf.

He is bigger than Tim. That's Mickey.

_______________ That's Susan.

_______________ That's _______________

2. Draw three matchstick people. Give them names. Ask your partner to compare them.

(Zeichne drei verschieden große Strichmännchen. Gib ihnen Namen. Laß deinen Partner/deine Partnerin ihre Größe vergleichen.)

a	b	c

(Zu den anderen Aufgaben sind mehrere Lösungen möglich. Zeige deinem Lehrer / deiner Lehrerin deine Lösungen. Er / Sie kann sie kontrollieren.)

A Jeans for me, please!

1. Work with a partner. You take part A, your partner takes part B. You are Tom.
(Lies das Gespräch mit einem Partner/einer Partnerin. Du bist Tom.)

No, Mum! Not these awful trousers.
No one in my class wears trousers like these.

Oh, Tom. Why do you always wear jeans?
Monday, Tuesday, Wednesday, Thursday, Friday, Saturday, Sunday.
You wear jeans every day.

But I like them. All young people like them.

Okay, jeans again then.
How about these?

Grey? I hate grey.

And these? They're blue.

Nearly everyone wears blue jeans.
Not for me.

Okay then. Here are some red jeans. Try them on.

Red? Red! Oh, Mum, they're great!
I think I'll take them.

2. *Jetzt könnt ihr die Rollen tauschen. Lest das Gespräch auf englisch ein zweites Mal. Dabei mußt du die deutschen Sätze ins Englische übersetzen. Dein Partner/Deine Partnerin kann dich kontrollieren und umgekehrt.*

3. *Übertrage die deutschen Sätze nun schriftlich ins Englische. Vergleiche zum Schluß mit dem Blatt deines Partners/deiner Partnerin.*

[4.] *Ihr könnt das Gespräch auswendig lernen und vor der Klasse spielen.*

CUT HERE

B Jeans for me, please!

1. Work with a partner. You take part B, your partner takes part A. You are Mum.
(Lies das Gespräch mit einem Partner/einer Partnerin. Du bist Mum.)

Nein, Mama. Nicht diese schreckliche Hose!
Niemand in meiner Klasse trägt solche Hosen.

Oh, Tom. Warum trägst du immer Jeans?
Montag, Dienstag, Mittwoch, Donnerstag, Freitag, Samstag, Sonntag.
Jeden Tag trägst du Jeans.

Aber mir gefallen sie. Alle jungen Leute mögen sie.

Also gut. Dann wieder Jeans. Wie wär's mit diesen?

Grau? Ich hasse grau.

Und diese da? Sie sind blau.

Fast jeder trägt blaue Jeans. Nicht für mich.

Also gut. Hier sind rote. Probier sie an.

Rot? Rot! Oh, Mama, sie sind toll!
Ich glaube, ich nehme sie.

2. *Jetzt könnt ihr die Rollen tauschen. Lest das Gespräch auf englisch ein zweites Mal. Dabei mußt du die deutschen Sätze ins Englische übersetzen. Dein Partner/Deine Partnerin kann dich kontrollieren und umgekehrt.*

3. *Übertrage die deutschen Sätze nun schriftlich ins Englische. Vergleiche zum Schluß mit dem Blatt deines Partners/deiner Partnerin.*

[4.] *Ihr könnt das Gespräch auswendig lernen und vor der Klasse spielen.*

Why? Why not?

1. Can you match the questions and the answers? Write the letters next to the numbers in the box. You don't need all the answers!
(Kannst du die Fragen und Antworten verbinden? Schreibe den richtigen Buchstaben zu der Zahl. Eine Antwort bleibt übrig!)

1) Tom always wears jeans. Why?
2) Today Linda is wearing a pullover and a cardigan. Why?
3) Susan looks funny in that dress. Why?
4) On weekdays Bobby wears trousers, a jacket and a tie. Why?
5) Ann doesn't want the new dress. Why not?
6) The Johnsons often order their clothes from a catalogue. Why?
7) Andy is looking for a new pullover. Why?
8) There's no school today. Why not?

a) Because it's not her size.
b) Because it's too big for her. It's her mother's.
c) Because he doesn't like other trousers.
d) Because they are looking for new clothes in the catalogue.
e) Because there's no shop in their village.
f) Because it's cold outside.
g) Because his old pullover is too small.
h) Because it's his school uniform.
i) Because it's Sunday.

1	c
2	f
3	b
4	h
5	a
6	e
7	g
8	i

2. Look at the pictures and answer the questions.

a) 

b) 

c) 

d) 

a) Boxer wants something to drink. Why?
Because he's thirsty.

b) Sally is very happy. Why?
Because it's her birthday.

c) William is going to bed. Why?
Because he is tired.

d) Patsy can't have a hamburger. Why not?
Because she hasn't got any money.

[3.] Can you write sentences now?
(Kannst du jetzt auch die Aussagen finden?)

a) 

b) 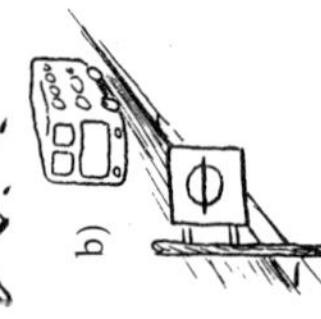

a) David can't watch TV. Why not?
Because he must do his homework.

b) Susy is running. Why?
Because the bus is coming.

The Slot Machine

go	went	gehen	ging
(have)	came	schreien	lebte
play	lived	bin	sagte
am	stopped	helfen	schrie
see	was	spielen	(hatte)
like	heard	zuschauen	mochte
watch	shouted	(haben)	stand auf
hear	played	versuchen	warst/waren
come	(had)	aufstehen	hörte
are	helped	rennen	spielte
help	liked	sehen	war
run	saw	bist/sind	sah
say	tried	mögen	half
live	watched	kommen	kam
stop	ran	hören	schaute zu
try	were	anhalten	rannte
get up	said	sagen	hielt an
shout	got up	leben	versuchte

Can you play with this slot machine? You win when you find four words which go together: Present and Past in English and German. Write them down in the table below.
(Kannst du an diesem Spielautomaten spielen? Du hast immer dann gewonnen, wenn du vier Wörter findest, die zusammenpassen: Gegenwart und Vergangenheit auf Englisch und auf Deutsch. Schreibe die Wörter in der Tabelle unten auf.)

have	had	haben	hatte
play	played	spielen	spielte
am	was	bin	war
see	saw	sehen	sah
like	liked	mögen	mochte
watch	watched	zuschauen	schaute zu
hear	heard	hören	hörte
come	came	kommen	kam
are	were	bist / sind	warst / waren
help	helped	helfen	half
run	ran	rennen	rannte
say	said	sagen	sagte
live	lived	leben	lebte
stop	stopped	anhalten	hielt an
try	tried	versuchen	versuchte
get up	got up	aufstehen	stand auf
shout	shouted	schreien	schrie

OUT IN THE CAR

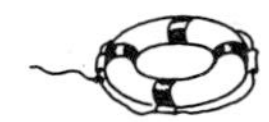

1. You can see all these things when you are out in the car. Write the English words in the puzzle to find out where Bob lives.
(Schreibe die englischen Wörter in das Puzzle um herauszufinden, wo Bob wohnt.)

1. A small town. village
2. The farmer lives here. farmhouse
3. You find cows and sheep in it. field
4. Cars drive on it. road
5. People live here. York is a town
6. You go from one side of the river to the other side across a bridge
7. Some people go there on Sunday. church
8. There is water in it, there are fish in it. river
9. You can see many cars in it. street
10. You park your car here. car park
11. The girl is pushing her bike up the hill
12. It's outside the house. There are flowers in it. You can play in it. garden

Bob lives in Great Britain

[2.] A word game. Who can make the most words?
Ihr braucht zwei Würfel. Wenn ihr zum Beispiel eine 3 und eine 4 werft, nehmt ihr die Lösungen von oben zu den Nummern 3 und 4 und zusätzlich zu der Nummer 7 (3 + 4). Jeder/Jede versucht für sich, aus den Buchstaben der drei Wörter so viele neue Wörter zu bilden, wie er/sie in drei Minuten schafft. Schaut in euren Englischbüchern nach, ob ihr alles richtig geschrieben habt! Wer die meisten Wörter schafft, hat gewonnen.

Beispiel: 3 = F I E L D 4 = R O A D 7 = C H U R C H

fall, record, folder, old, here, dear, café, card, ...

FOLD HERE

You can find the answers to the puzzle here. Colour the words in.

BRIDGETUBCARPARKETCCHURCHBGE
FARMHOUSEKANFIELDPOTGARDENTMLHILL
RIVERIFEROADFASTREETRETOWNXLVILLAGE

Mark is very busy in April. **13 APRIL** Here is a list of things he has got to do.

Monday, April 1st: go shopping with Dad
Tuesday, April 2nd: play tennis with Sally
Wednesday, April 3rd: work in Mr Benson's garden
Thursday, April 4th: look at Tim's postcard collection
Friday, April 5th: clean my bike
Saturday, April 6th: help Dad in the garage
Sunday, April 7th: go to the cinema
Monday, April 8th: play volleyball at the sports club
Tuesday, April 9th: have lunch with Aunt Sally
Wednesday, April 10th: stay at home and learn for my German test
Thursday, April 11th: take Mr Nesbit's dog for a walk
Friday, April 12th: see Tom in town

Now it's April 13th.

1. Here are some pages out of Mark's diary. Write the correct days and dates on each page.

(Es ist nun der 13. April. Hier sind einige Seiten aus Marks Tagebuch. Trage die Tage und Daten ein.)

Monday	Thursday	Sunday	Friday
I played volleyball.	I looked at Tim's postcards.	I went to the cinema.	I cleaned my bike.
April 8th	April 4th	April 7th	April 5th

2. You are Mark. Write down what you did each day.

Tuesday	Saturday	Tuesday	Thursday
I played tennis with Sally.	I helped Dad in the garage.	I had lunch with Aunt Sally.	I took Mr Nesbit's dog for a walk.
April 2nd	**April 6th**	**April 9th**	**April 11th**

3. Answer the questions about Mark.

a) What did he do yesterday? He saw Tom in town.
b) What did he do last Friday? He cleaned his bike.
c) What did he do ten days ago? He worked in Mr Benson's garden.
d) What did he do last weekend? He helped in the garage and went to the cinema.
e) What did he do last Wednesday? He stayed at home and learned for his German test.
f) What did he do four days ago? He had lunch with Aunt Sally.

What's wrong here?

Julia's typewriter was broken, when she wrote this story.
Can you correct the text?

```
Yes terdaywa sa veryex citingday fo r me. I twas Mart in's
birth da y, soIwe nt toh is hou se, be causeth erew asa
b igpar ty. Ma rt inopenedt he dooran dsaid: "Hello, Ju lia,
nicetoseeyou, co mein." All the o therteena gers we re
alr eadyatt hepa rty, whenIca mein. Isa id 'hello' toeve ry-
body. Martinha d a rec ord pl ayeran d ma n yre cor ds. So
wel ist ened toso me po p music. The rewa s tha t grea told
so ng by ACDC. "C om eon, ev erybody", shout edMartin,
"le t'sda nce." T hemu sic was fan tastica nd ev erybody
wa shap pyand dan ced. Atn ine o'cl ock Ma rtin's mo ther
camein a ndsa id: "Chi ldren, it'sti me togoh ome now. O ne
mor erecorda nd thepa rtyis over." Mar tinand Ida ncedt he
la stda nce together. Iwa s veryha ppy, be cau seM art in
sa idto me: " I real lyli keyou."
```

Yesterday was a very exciting day for me. It was Martin's birthday, so I went to his house, because there was a big party. Martin opened the door and said: "Hello, Julia, nice to see you, come in." All the other teenagers were already at the party, when I came in. I said 'hello' to everybody. Martin had a record player and many records. So we listened to some pop music. There was that great old song by ACDC. "Come on, everybody," shouted Martin, "let's dance." The music was fantastic and everybody was happy and danced. At nine o'clock Martin's mother came in and said: "Children, it's time to go home now. One more record and the party is over." Martin and I danced the last dance together. I was very happy, because Martin said to me: "I really like you."

Talking to grandma

One day after school last week John went to visit his grandma.

Grandma: Oh, it's you, John. Come in. Let's have a cup of tea and a chocolate biscuit together!
John: Yes, please, I'm hungry!
Grandma: You're always hungry! What did you do at school today?
John: We're learning about our village 50 years ago. Miss Stanley told us to find out about the village. Can you tell me something about it, Grandma? Have you got any old photos?
Grandma: Let me see. Yes, I think I have got some photographs. Look on the bookshelf in the living room. There's a big blue album. Bring it here and we can look together.
John: Here it is, Grandma.
Grandma: The village was very quiet 50 years ago.
John: Yes, there were no cars in the street – just bikes!
Grandma: That's right. We all rode bicycles then – not just the children! And look at this picture. That was Mr Harper's shop. He had a little shop at the corner.
John: Is that where the supermarket is now?
Grandma: Yes. When I was young there was no supermarket, everyone went to Mr Harper's to do their shopping. And look, this is me and my brothers. There were lots of big trees where the car park is now. We often played there. We had our own tree house.
John: The village was much greener then, and much cleaner! Who's this in the river?
Grandma: Oh, that's your grandpa. He often went swimming in the river!
John: Was the river clean?
Grandma: Yes, it was very clean. There were a lot of fish in it, too. We often went fishing and had fresh fish for tea.
John: Everything is different here now.
Grandma: Well, not everything is gone. Look at this picture. The church is still the same as it was 50 years ago!
John: Oh, yes! And that's you and grandpa in front of the church. You looked fantastic!
Grandma: Yes, and look! We only had a small tree in our garden 50 years ago! Now the same tree is taller than the house!
John: The village was very nice 50 years ago. Do you still like it now?
Grandma: Yes, I do. It's different now, but it's still very nice. And I'm always very happy when you come for tea!

Now and then

1. Now the village is noisy. Then it was quiet.
2. Now there are a lot of cars. Then everyone rode bikes.
3. Now there is a supermarket. Then Mr Harper had a little shop at the corner.
4. Now there is a car park. Then there were lots of big trees.
5. Now the river is dirty. Then it was clean.
6. Now there is a big tree in grandma's garden. Then the tree was very small.

Jobs in the house

Across:

4 I can't play with you. I've got to do some jobs in the house.

14 There's a hole in the box.

16 You've got to repair the box.

18 A hammer is a tool.

19 This pencil is broken.

Down:

15 Where's the toaster? I want to make some toast.

FOLD HERE

You can find the answers here:

GLUEWOODELECTRICSAWPAINTBRUSHSCREWDRIVERPAPERDOORHAMMERMAKE
BOOKSHELFPAINTTOOLBROKENELECTRICDRILLREPAIRNAILHOLEJOBS

Did you use . . . ?

Randy has got a nice collection of postcards. Last Saturday he made a box for his postcards.

What did he need to make the box?

He needed paint, a paint brush, glue, paper and scissors.

Today Randy's Mum wants to do some jobs in the house. She needs many things but she can't find them. So she asks Randy:

1 *Did you use the* saw ? *No, I didn't.*
2 *Did you use the* green paint ? *Yes, I did.*
3 Did you use the hammer ? No, I didn't .
4 Did you use the paint brush ? Yes, I did .
5 Did you use any nails ? No, I didn't .
6 Did you use any screws ? No, I didn't .
7 Did you use a screwdriver ? No, I didn't .
8 Did you use the scissors ? Yes, I did .

What jobs did they do?

It was 9.00 on Saturday morning. The Bells had a lot of jobs to do.

Everyone helped.

Two hours later . . .

1. Answer please.

a) Did Mrs Bell clean the car? *Yes,* she did.
b) Did Gran wash up? No, she didn't.
c) Did Mr Bell wash the trousers? Yes, he did.
d) Did Aunt Linda go shopping? No, she didn't.
e) Did Ben repair the clock? No, he didn't.
f) Did Ellen put up the picture? No, she didn't.
g) Did Ben make the beds? No, he didn't.

No, he didn't.
No, she didn't.
Yes, he did.
Yes, she did.

2. Make three more questions:

a) (Zeige deinem Lehrer / deiner Lehrerin deine Fragen.
b) Er / Sie wird sie kontrollieren.)
c)

3. Now write down who did what. (Eine andere Reihenfolge ist möglich.)

a) *Mrs Bell cleaned the car.*
b) Mr Bell put up the picture.
c) Gran made the beds.
d) Ellen washed up.
e) Mr Bell washed the trousers.
f) Aunt Linda repaired the clock.
g) Ben went shopping.

Jobs for Sally and Alice

Mrs Miller is a shop assistant. Last Saturday she was at work so she made a list of jobs for Sally and Alice to do.

You wash up! I don't like washing up.

O.K., but you can make the beds then!

Yes, and I want to clean out the bird cage.

And I'd like to wash the kitchen floor. Can you help me to clean up the living room?

All right, and let's do the shopping together. After that we can repair Mum's bike. Do you want to telephone Gran?

Why not? I like Gran!

1. What did Sally and Alice each want to do?

Sally wanted to make the beds.

She wanted to clean out the bird cage.

Alice wanted to wash up.

She wanted to wash the kitchen floor.

She wanted to telephone Gran.

Sally and Alice wanted to clean up the living room.

They wanted to do the shopping together

They wanted to repair Mum's bike.

2. Sally and Alice worked hard. What did they do? Use the words in the box.

washed	cleaned	made	did	telephoned	repaired

Sally *made the beds.*

She cleaned out the bird cage.

Alice washed up.

She washed the kitchen floor.

She telephoned Gran.

Sally and Alice cleaned up the living room.

They did the shopping together.

They repaired Mum's bike.

Roy's plans for the weekend

1. What did Roy want to do at the weekend?

a) *He wanted to work for his English test.*

b) *He wanted to* play tennis.

c) He wanted to watch television.

d) He wanted to paint a picture.

e) He wanted to play football.

f) He wanted to go swimming.

g) He wanted to listen to his records.

h) He wanted to play table-tennis.

But then on Friday morning

2. What **didn't** Roy do at the weekend?

He didn't play tennis.

He didn't play football.

He didn't go swimming.

He didn't play table-tennis.

3. What **did** Roy do at the weekend?

He worked for his English test.

He watched television.

He painted a picture.

He listened to his records.

[4.] You can link two sentences. Use "but". Make four new sentences.
(Du kannst zwei Sätze mit Hilfe von "but" verbinden. Bilde vier neue Sätze.)

He worked for his English test, but he didn't play tennis.

He watched television, but he didn't play football.

He painted a picture, but he didn't go swimming.

He listened to his records, but he didn't play table-tennis.

A telephone call

It's Sunday afternoon.
The telephone in the Browns' flat is ringing.

Martin: Manchester 63074. Martin Brown speaking.
Mandy: Hello, Martin. It's me, Mandy. I want to go to the cinema at 6.00. Do you want to come?
Martin: I'd like to come. But I can't. There's no bus before 7.00. And I can't go by bike. My bike is broken.
Mandy: Why didn't you repair it yesterday?
Martin: I didn't have the right tools.
Mandy: What did you do yesterday?
Martin: I helped my dad in the garden and did the shopping. What did you do yesterday?
Mandy: Oh, I went to my uncle's farm. It was great.
Martin: Did you have a ride on the pony?
Mandy: Yes, it was good fun. Perhaps you can come with me next weekend.
Martin: Yes, that's a good idea. Listen, why don't you come here this evening? I bought a new record yesterday. We can listen to it and make some plans for the weekend.
Mandy: O.K. See you later. Bye.
Martin: Bye.

1. Read the dialogue with a partner.

2. Write a new dialogue. Change the sentences above which are underlined. Use the sentences below.
(Schreibe ein neues Gespräch. Anstelle der Sätze im Text oben, die unterstrichen sind, setze die Sätze unten richtig ein.)

- Oh, I was at the sports centre.
- I didn't have time.
- I want to see Tim and Sally at the coffee shop at 6.00.
- I washed our car and helped with the housework.
- Why didn't you take it to the bike shop yesterday?
- Did you go roller skating?

Martin: Manchester 63074. Martin Brown speaking.
Mandy: Hello, Martin. It's me, Mandy. *I want to see* Tim and Sally at the coffee shop at 6.00. Do you want to come?
Martin: I'd like to come. But I can't. There's no bus before 7.00. And I can't go by bike. My bike is broken.
Mandy: Why didn't you take it to the bike shop yesterday?
Martin: I didn't have time.
Mandy: What did you do yesterday?
Martin: I washed our car and helped with the housework. What did you do yesterday?
Mandy: Oh, I was at the sports centre. It was great.
Martin: Did you go roller skating?
Mandy: Yes, it was good fun. Perhaps you can come with me next weekend.
Martin: Yes, that's a good idea. Listen, why don't you all come here this evening? I bought a new record yesterday. We can listen to it and make some plans for the weekend.
Mandy: O.K. See you later. Bye.
Martin: Bye.

An accident

Yesterday John saw an accident.
Later he talked to a policeman.

1. What did the policeman ask him?

Did you see the accident?	Yes, I saw the accident.
Did he come down Queen Street ?	No, he came down King Street.
Did he turn left ?	No, he didn't turn left. He turned right.
Did a cat run across the street ?	No, a dog ran across the street.
Did he see the dog ?	Yes, he saw the dog.
Did he try to stop ?	Yes, he tried to stop.
Did you telephone the police ?	No, I didn't. A woman telephoned the police.
Did the dog run away ?	Yes, the dog ran away.
Do you know whose dog it was ?	I think it was the Millers' dog.

2. Alan's accident. Join the sentences in the right order.

- Yesterday Alan went for a ride on his bike.
- He fell off his bike.
- A woman telephoned the police and a doctor.
- Alan saw the dog and tried to stop.
- At that moment a big brown dog ran across the road.
- But it was too late.
- He wanted to go and see his friend Brian in Queen Street.
- He went down King Street and turned right into Queen Street.

FOLD HERE

Here are the policeman's questions:

Did he turn left? – Did he try to stop? – Did he come down Queen Street? – Did the dog run away?
Did he see the dog? – Did you telephone the police? – Did a cat run across the street?
~~Did you see the accident?~~ – Do you know whose dog it was?

When do the trains leave?

DEPARTURES	
9.25	London
9.43	Sheffield
9.50	York
10.05	Brighton
10.15	Dover
11.22	Birmingham

When does the train to London leave?
At twenty-five past nine.
And what's the time now?
It's five past nine.
Oh, good. Enough time for a cup of tea.

1. Complete the short dialogues. *(Schreibe die kurzen Gespräche auf.)*

When does the train to Sheffield leave?
At nine forty-three.
And what's the time now?
It's twenty past nine.
Oh, good. Enough time for a piece of cake.

When does the train to York leave?
At nine fifty.
And what's the time now?
It's nine twenty-five.
Oh, good. Enough time for a hamburger.

When does the train to Birmingham leave?
At eleven twenty-two.
And what's the time now?
It's twenty-five to eleven.
Oh, good. Enough time for an ice-cream.

[2.] Practise the dialogues with a partner.

Bad luck!

Tom — Andy

1. What does Andy say? Answer Tom's questions.

Hello, Andy. I tried to phone you yesterday. Where were you?
I was out in the afternoon.
What did you do?
a) I went to town.
How did you get there?
b) I went by bike.
Why did you go there?
c) Because I needed some new batteries for my walkman.
Where did you buy them?
d) I bought them at Rod's Radio Shop.
When did you come home again?
e) I came home at five o'clock.
And what did you do then?
f) I listened to the Tigers on my walkman.
But I phoned again at about 5.30.
I didn't hear the telephone. The music was so good!
Bad luck! I had a ticket for the Tigers' concert for you! I went there last night.

2. Now write about Andy's afternoon.

He was out in the afternoon. He went to town. He went by bike.
He needed some new batteries for his walkman.
He bought them at Rod's Radio Shop.
He came home at five o'clock.
He listened to the Tigers on his walkman.

[3.] Practise the dialogue with your partner.

[4.] Ask your partner about Andy.

a) Where was Andy yesterday?
b) What did he do?
c) How did he ...?
d) Why did he ...?
e) Where did he ...?
f) When did he ...?
g) What did he ...?
h) Why didn't he ...?

FOLD HERE

Here are Andy's answers:
Because I needed some new batteries for my walkman. / I went by bike. / I came home at five o'clock. / I went to town. / I bought them at Rod's Radio Shop. / I listened to the Tigers on my walkman.

? ? ? ? What? ??? ? ? ? How? ? ? ? Why? When? ? ? ? ? Where? ? ? ? ?

1. Fill in the right question word: What – How – When – Why – Where.

When	did you go to the village?	At 2.30.
What	did you buy there?	Some eggs.
Where	did you buy them?	At the supermarket.
Why	did you need eggs?	Because I wanted to make a cake.
What	did you do in the evening?	I watched television.
When	did you go to bed?	At about half past ten.
Why	didn't you go to bed earlier?	Because my parents were out!

2. Make questions out of these sentences. *(Bilde Fragen zu diesen Sätzen.)*

a) What did you buy yesterday? Yesterday I bought a new calculator.

b) Why did you need a new calculator?
I needed a new calculator because my old one is broken.

c) How much did it cost?
It cost £ 12.

d) Where did you go in the evening?
I went to the cinema in the evening.

e) What did you see?
I saw Rocky XXI.

f) When did it finish?
It finished at ten o'clock.

g) How did you get / go home?
I went home by train.

[3.] Write the questions in English and ask your partner to answer them.
(Schreibe diese Fragen auf englisch und stelle sie deinem Partner/deiner Partnerin.)

Ask your partner:

- *wann er/sie gestern heimkam.*
- *was er/sie nach der Schule tat.*
- *warum er/sie nicht anrief.*
- *wann er/sie gestern ins Bett ging.*
- *wie er/sie heute zur Schule kam.*

When did you come home yesterday?
What did you do after school?
Why didn't you telephone?
When did you go to bed yesterday?
How did you come to school today?

Time to get up

When do these people get up? When do they start work? What are their jobs?

 4:30 He gets up at three. He starts work at four thirty. He's a greengrocer.	 3:00 He gets up at two. He starts work at three. He's a baker.	 10:00 He gets up at eight. He starts work at ten. He's a policeman.
 5:00 He gets up at three. He starts work at five. He's a nurse.	 6:30 She gets up at five. She starts work at six thirty. She's a driver.	 8:00 He gets up at seven. He starts work at eight. He's a pupil.
 9:00 He gets up at seven thirty. He starts work at nine. He's an office worker.	 22:00 He gets up at two. He starts work at ten. He's a miner.	 19:30 He gets up at one. He starts work at seven thirty. He's a clown.

Who is it?

A game for two people

Prägt euch zuerst die Bilder und Angaben genau ein.
Dann stellst du deinem Partner/deiner Partnerin zehn Fragen, die mit „Who" beginnen.
Dein Partner/Deine Partnerin versucht, die richtigen Antworten zu geben, ohne die Bilder anzuschauen.
Beispiel: Who gets up at two o'clock? That's the baker.
Who starts work at seven thirty? That's the clown.

Für jede richtige Antwort gibt es einen Punkt.
Nun stellt dein Partner/deine Partnerin dir zehn Fragen. Wer die meisten Punkte erreicht, hat gewonnen.

FOLD HERE

These words will help you:

GREENGROCERPOLICEMANPUPILCLERKMINERNURSEBAKERDRIVERCLOWN

Word families

1. Make word families. Join the words that go together. *(Bilde Wortfamilien. Verbinde die zusammengehörigen Wörter.)*

talk	town hall	tomato	foggy
plate	flower	Italian	grass
blue	speak	green	station
potato	rainy	saucer	say
shirt	morning	shop	bean
prison	cup	bottle	blouse
bag	trousers	tree	glass
plant	yellow	tell	Spanish
windy	French	skirt	night
Greek	lettuce	cloudy	pot
evening	basket	afternoon	orange
fork	outside	watch	mouth
eye	teacher	sandwich	juice
coffee	hot	spoon	cold
driver	Greece	lemonade	inside
biscuits	look	nose	Italy
opposite	knife	thirsty	magazine
hungry	toast	mechanic	bread
see	tea	across	football
Germany	ear	tennis	notice
skating	comic	Spain	tea spoon
book	swimming	newspaper	shop assistant

2. Now it's your turn. Make your own word families. *(Bilde deine eigenen Wortfamilien.)*

a) bus — van — car — coach

b) rabbit — dog — cat — hamster

c) (Zeige deinem Lehrer/deiner Lehrerin deine Lösung.)

[3.] *Spielt zu zweit. Zuerst falte ein Blatt, so daß 16 Felder entstehen. Nun schreibe die Wörter von vier Wortfamilien in die Felder, wobei jedes Feld nur ein Wort enthält. Jetzt hast du 16 Wortkärtchen. Schneide die Kärtchen aus. Mische deine Kärtchen mit den Kärtchen deines Partners/deiner Partnerin und lege alle Kärtchen mit der beschrifteten Seite nach unten auf den Tisch. Jeder/Jede darf nun der Reihe nach vier Kärtchen umdrehen. Versucht dabei die Wortfamilien wiederzufinden. Wer findet zuerst vier Familien?*

The adjectives page

1. Join the English and German words. They are all adjectives. *(Verbinde die englischen und deutschen Wörter. Sie sind alle Adjektive.)*

angry	*schön*	full	*glücklich*
awful	*klug*	funny	*heiß*
bad	*tot*	hairy	*interessant*
beautiful	*gefährlich*	happy	*nett*
big	*ärgerlich*	heavy	*reich*
clever	*schlimm*	hot	*voll*
cloudy	*schrecklich*	hungry	*spät*
dangerous	*früh*	interesting	*lustig*
dead	*gerecht*	late	*süß*
difficult	*groß*	little	*behaart*
early	*schnell*	nice	*schwer*
easy	*wolkig*	poor	*langsam*
empty	*umsonst*	rich	*hungrig*
fair	*schwierig*	slow	*klein*
fast	*leer*	sweet	*durstig*
free	*leicht*	thirsty	*arm*

2. Fill in the missing adjectives. *(Vervollständige die Adjektive.)*

a difficult test

an angry teacher

an empty bottle

the cloudy sky

a slow car

an interesting story

[3.] Draw these pictures in your exercise book: a) a happy girl b) a hairy monster c) a funny face.

MacDougall and MacDuff

Last summer holidays MacDougall and MacDuff went to England. They had a nice holiday. Look where they went and how they travelled.

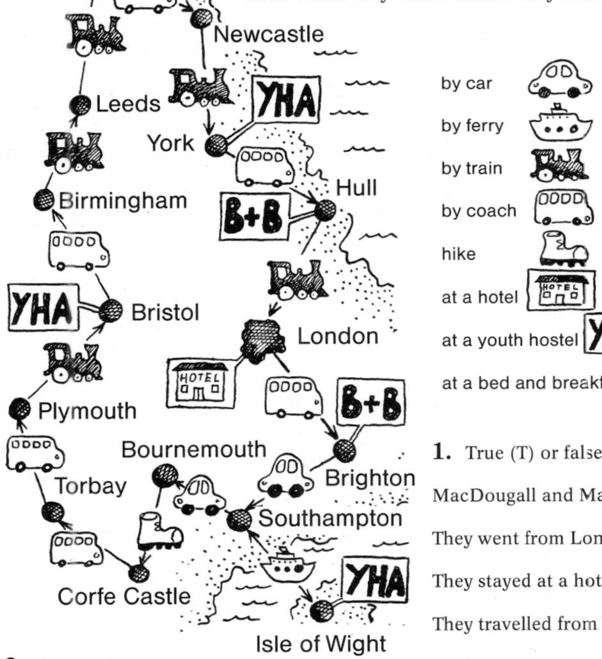

1. True (T) or false (F)? *(Richtig* (T) *oder falsch* (F)?)

	T/F
MacDougall and MacDuff went to Newcastle by train.	F
They went from London to Brighton by bus.	T
They stayed at a hotel in London and in Bristol.	F
They travelled from York to Hull by car.	F

2. Answer the questions.

How did MacDougall and MacDuff get from Edinburgh to York? *By coach and by* train.

How did they get from London to Brighton? By coach.

How did they get from Brighton to Southampton? By car.

How did they get from Southampton to the Isle of Wight? By ferry.

How did they get from Bournemouth to Corfe Castle? *They* hiked.

Where did they stay in London? *At a* hotel.

Where did they stay in Brighton? At a bed and breakfast place.

Where did they stay in Bristol? At a youth hostel.

3. Write three new sentences about MacDougall's and MacDuff's holiday.

They went from Torbay *to* Plymouth *by* coach.

They went from Birmingham *to* Leeds *by* train.

In York *they stayed at a* youth hostel.

(Andere Lösungen sind auch möglich.)

[4.] *Laß deinen Partner/deine Partnerin das Bild eine Minute lang anschauen. Danach stellst du ihm/ihr fünf „True/False"-Aufgaben. Dein Partner/deine Partnerin muß antworten, ohne das Bild anzuschauen! Dann geht es umgekehrt. Wer gibt die meisten richtigen Antworten?*

Mum's photo box

One evening Mum opens her photo box. The children are very interested in the old photos.

1. Can you find the right sentences? Mark them with a tick (✓).

Mum was a good pupil.	✓	Dad was a good sportsman.	✓
She met Dad at a school fete.		He met Mum 21 years ago.	
She didn't like Dad at first.		He was once in a funny play with Mum.	✓
She married Dad 31 years ago.			

2. Can you answer the questions?

When did the school circus start every year?
It started in June.

Where did Mum and Dad meet?
They met at the circus.

What did Dad and his partner do in the circus?
They did tricks on their bikes.

Did the grandparents like Dad at first?
No, they didn't.

Why did people laugh at Mum and Dad?
Because they were very funny. They were clowns.

THE WEATHER

1. Find the 16 "weather" words in this word square. Write them down here:

B	E	A	K	L	T	C	L	O	U	D	Y
E	F	G	C	O	L	D	H	Y	S	T	U
A	W	F	U	L	R	T	F	O	G	G	Y
U	M	O	T	H	R	E	Z	S	H	L	K
T	H	U	N	D	E	R	S	T	O	R	M
I	S	V	I	X	L	R	U	O	T	T	W
F	H	A	C	O	N	I	N	R	P	O	T
U	O	C	E	B	R	B	N	M	W	R	D
L	W	A	P	E	N	L	Y	Y	I	N	F
D	E	T	H	O	U	E	K	N	N	Q	I
O	R	S	N	O	W	Y	R	S	D	T	N
G	Y	N	O	T	R	A	I	N	Y	G	E

1) nice
2) thunderstorm
3) beautiful
4) terrible
5) showery
6) cloudy
7) stormy
8) snowy
9) sunny
10) hot
11) cold
12) fine
13) windy
14) foggy
15) rainy
16) awful

2. What's the weather like? Choose words from the word square and write them next to the pictures.

1 windy, rainy, terrible, awful

2 hot, sunny, fine, beautiful, nice

3 thunderstorm, stormy, terrible

4 foggy, cold

5 snowy, cold

6 rainy, cloudy, terrible

Weather Report

Read the weather report, then cut out the symbols at the bottom of the page and stick them in the right places.
(Schneide die Wettersymbole unten aus und klebe sie an die richtigen Stellen in der Wetterkarte.)

Spot the difference

1. What is different in picture 2? Mark the differences in picture 2 with a cross (x).
(Was ist anders? Markiere die Unterschiede im Bild 2 mit einem Kreuz (x).)

1

2

2. Write down what you can see in the pictures.

a) *door*
b) picture
c) notice board
d) ceiling
e) window
f) plants
g) poster
h) books
i) wall
j) clock
k) map
l) board
m) desk
n) ruler
o) pen
p) chair
q) school bag
r) tank
s) cage
t) cupboard
u) shelves

[3.] Write about the differences in your exercise book.

Example: *In picture 1 there's a map of England but in picture 2 there's a map of Germany.*

• • • • • • • • • • • • • • • • **FOLD HERE** • • • • • • • • • • • • • • • • • • •

Here are the things you can see in the picture:

NOTICEBOARDDOORCEILINGWINDOWPICTURESPENCHAIRSCUPBOARDSHELVES
MAPSCHOOLBAGSWALLPOSTERSDESKSPLANTSBOARDRULERCAGETANKCLOCKBOOKS

NEXT WEEKEND

1. What are these people going to do next weekend? Write down who says what.
(Was machen diese Leute am Wochenende? Schreibe auf, wer was sagt.)

Tom : I'm going to make some shelves.
Bob : I'm going to see Robin Hood at the cinema.
Mary : I'm going to go to a bike race.
Ann : I'm going to meet Pedro at the circus.
Carol : I'm going to help in the garden.
Mike : I'm going to watch the Punch & Judy show.
Cindy and Dave : We're going to see our grandmother.
The Bakers : We're going to go on a boat trip.

2. Now draw a picture and write a sentence about yourself.

You: *I'm going to* ______.

He's / *She's* / *They're* — *going to ...*

3. Answer the questions.

What's Tom going to do next weekend?
He's going to make some shelves.

What's Mike going to do next weekend?
He's going to watch the Punch and Judy show.

What's Ann going to do next weekend?
She's going to meet Pedro at the circus.

What are Cindy and Dave going to do next weekend?
They're going to see their grandmother.

What's Carol going to do next weekend?
She's going to help in the garden.

What are the Bakers going to do next weekend?
They're going to go on a boat trip.

Make a picture.
Cut out the squares at the bottom and stick them on the correct dates.

A PUZZLE

Schneide die Kärtchen unten aus und klebe sie auf die richtigen Daten im oberen Kästchen. Wenn du alles richtig machst, erkennst du ein Bild.

Example: 10.4 means the tenth day of the fourth month: April. So the answer is: the tenth of April.

A CROSSWORD PUZZLE

Put in the English words:

DOWN ↓

1 *sein, seine*
2 *Platz, Sitz*
3 *Gras*
4 *(zer)brechen*
5 *stricken*
7 *Gartenarbeit*
8 *Kosten*
10 *Fahrplan*
12 *aufgeregt*
14 *schwierig*
17 *Freund*
18 *Modell*
20 *Gitarre*
22 *überall*
26 *Strand*
27 *Netzball*
28 *früh*
31 *jung*
32 *auch*

ACROSS →

3 *Garten*
6 *Ei*
9 *Sohn*
11 *bevor*
13 *interessant*
15 *schneiden*
16 *frei, kostenlos*
19 *zusammen*
21 *Lieblings-*
23 *Männer*
24 *Käfig*
25 *spät*
29 *Fluß*
30 *Eisenbahn*
32 *Telefon*
33 *Garage*
34 *laufen*
35 *Flugzeug*
36 *sammeln*

• • • • • • • • • • • • • • • • • • • **FOLD HERE** • • • • • • • • • • • • • • • • • • •

Here are the English words:

his son knit interesting seat egg gardening favourite difficult cage early collect netball plane too free before guitar men grass garden timetable together late excited friend break model river garage run everyone cost telephone young railway cut

Pat's hobbies

What does Pat collect?
Connect the German words with the right English words. Use a ruler. Each line goes through one letter. Put the letters in the right place in the box below to answer the question.

Verbinde die zusammengehörigen deutschen und englischen Wörter mit einem Lineal. Jede Linie durchkreuzt so einen Buchstaben. Um die Frage beantworten zu können, mußt du jeden Buchstaben an der richtigen Stelle in die Kästchen unten einsetzen.

2	*interessant*	mustn't
11	*zeigen*	gardening
1	*nicht dürfen*	beach
3	*Gartenarbeit*	difficult
5	*während*	railway
9	*Kaugummi*	together
6	*Eisenbahn*	notice
10	*Briefmarke*	while
8	*schwierig*	chewing gum
7	*zusammen*	windy
13	*windig*	stamp
12	*Notiz*	show
4	*Strand*	cut
14	*schneiden*	interesting
16	*Gitarre*	collect
15	*sammeln*	hope
18	*verpassen*	knit
20	*Wetter*	guitar
17	*stricken*	miss
21	*warm*	warm
19	*hoffen*	weather

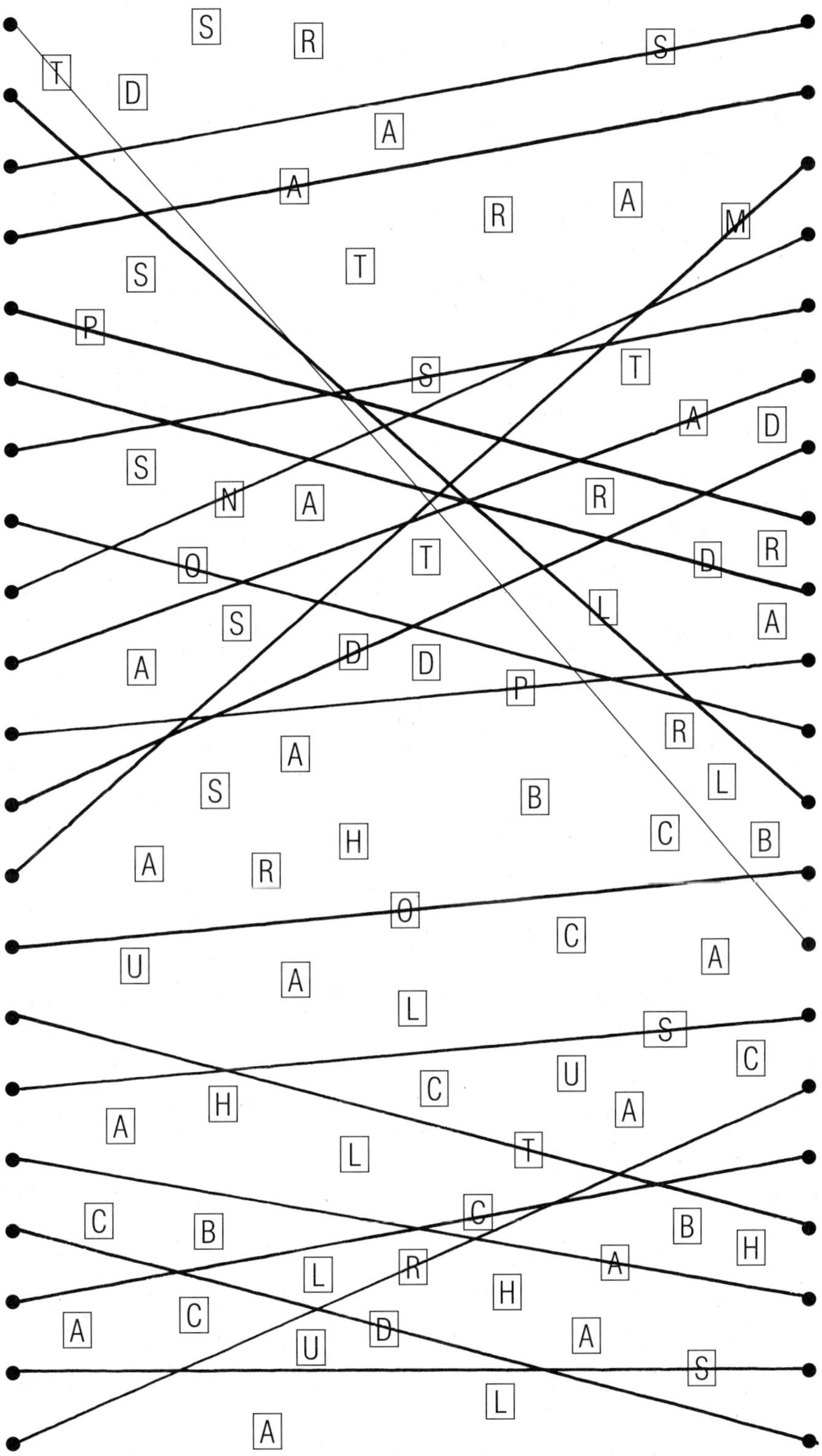

Pat collects

1	2	3	4	5	6	7	8	9	10	11	12	13	14	15	16	17	18	19	20	21
S	T	A	M	P	S	A	N	D	O	L	D	P	O	S	T	C	A	R	D	S

Hobbies

1. Here are some "hobby flowers". Can you write the hobbies from the box in the petals of the flowers? *(Hier sind einige „Hobby-Blumen". Kannst du die Hobbies aus dem Kästchen in die Blätter der passenden Blumen schreiben?)*

model planes	swimming	a cat	tennis	stamps	postcards	netball	the guitar	books
socks	photos	old things	model cars	ice-skating	comics	a dog		
~~football~~	fishing	pullovers	dancing	a rabbit	pets	riding	model boats	magazines

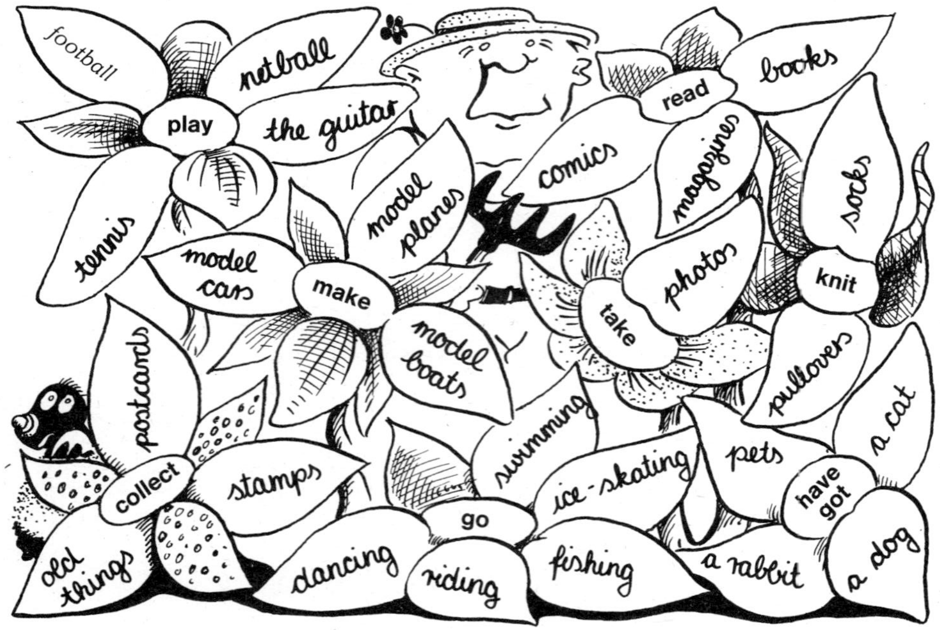

2. Make sentences about people and their hobbies. Use the words from the flowers.

Some people play football.

Mum collects stamps.

Peter plays tennis.

Sarah makes model planes.

Alan and Kate have got a cat.

(Zeige deinem Lehrer / deiner Lehrerin deine Lösungen. Andere Lösungen sind möglich.)

[3.] Make a "hobby flower" and hang it up in your classroom.

Free Time

1. Read the text about what Alan does in his free time. Then complete the table. *(Lies den Text über Alans Freizeit. Dann vervollständige die Tabelle.)*

In his free time Alan plays football. He isn't in a sports club. He likes pop music. He plays the piano. His favourite group is "Simple Minds". He has got fifteen records and eight cassettes. He reads books about stamps. He collects German stamps. He sometimes goes for bike rides. He watches television for an hour a day. He hasn't got a computer.

	Alan	Linda	you
Sport	football	volleyball	
Sports club	no	no	
Music	pop music	pop music	
Instrument	piano	guitar	
Favourite singer/group	Simple Minds	Bonnie Tyler	
Records	15	20	
Cassettes	8	12	
Reading	books about stamps	magazines	
Collection	German stamps	star photos	
Bike riding	sometimes	often	
Television	1 hour a day	2 hours a day	
Computer	no	yes	

2. Look at the table and write sentences about what Linda does in her free time. *(Schreibe nun einen Text über Lindas Freizeit.)*

In her free time Linda plays volleyball. She isn't in a sports club. She likes pop music. She plays the guitar. Her favourite singer is Bonnie Tyler. She has got 20 records and 12 cassettes. She reads magazines. She collects star photos. She often goes for bike rides. She watches television for 2 hours a day. She has got a computer.

3. And you? What do you do in your free time? Fill in the table and write some sentences.

In my free time I play

(Zeige deinem Lehrer / deiner Lehrerin deine Lösung.)

I think I'll ... ~ I don't think I'll ...

What are they saying?

Don't – it's not allowed!

1. Look at the signs. Now put the letters next to the right sentences.

a	Don't play football in the car park.
h	Don't bring your dog into the supermarket.
g	Don't write on the wall.
d	Don't fish in this river.
c	Don't pick the flowers in the park.
b	Don't eat ice-cream in the clothes shop.
e	Don't ride your bike in the playground.
f	Don't feed the animals at the zoo.

2. You mustn't . . . . Write sentences to go with the signs.

a) *You mustn't play football in the car park.*
b) *You mustn't* eat ice-cream in the clothes shop.
c) You mustn't pick the flowers in the park.
d) You mustn't fish in this river.
e) You mustn't ride your bike in the playground.
f) You mustn't feed the animals at the zoo.
g) You mustn't write on the wall.
h) You mustn't bring your dog into the supermarket.

[3.] Can you draw signs for these sentences? *(Kannst du zu diesen Sätzen Schilder zeichnen?)*
You mustn't swim in the river. Don't cross the road here.

Growing Words

Grow your own new words! Just add one letter to the word given.
(Bilde neue Wörter. Du brauchst nur einen weiteren Buchstaben zu dem gegebenen Wort hinzuzufügen. Manchmal mußt du den neuen Buchstaben am Anfang, manchmal in der Mitte und manchmal am Ende des gegebenen Wortes hinzufügen.)

Example: READ + B = BREAD

Here are the new words in German: *anfangen, Anzug, Ball, Bauernhof, bringen, ~~Brot,~~ buchstabieren, drei, eins, Eisenbahn, Fahrer, Flugzeug, haarig, Hand, hören, jeder, kalt, Lied, Mäuse, Mutter, Regen, Sand, schicken, sie, Sitz, spielen, Stuhl, Stunde, Teller, tot, tragen, Uhr, warm, waschen, weg, wissen, wo, zeigen*

A Don't miss the bus!

You are at the bus stop after school with your friend.

1. Work with a partner. You take part A, your partner takes part B. You are Kevin.
(Lies das Gespräch mit einem Partner/einer Partnerin. Du bist Kevin.)

2. *Jetzt könnt ihr die Rollen tauschen. Lest das Gespräch auf englisch ein zweites Mal. Dabei mußt du die deutschen Sätze ins Englische übersetzen. Dein Partner/Deine Partnerin kann dich kontrollieren und umgekehrt.*

3. *Übertrage die deutschen Sätze nun schriftlich ins Englische. Vergleiche zum Schluß mit dem Blatt deines Partners/deiner Partnerin.*

[4.] *Ihr könnt das Gespräch auswendig lernen und vor der Klasse spielen.*

CUT HERE

B Don't miss the bus!

You are at the bus stop after school with your friend.

1. Work with a partner. You take part B, your partner takes part A. You are Tracey.
(Lies das Gespräch mit einem Partner/einer Partnerin. Du bist Tracey.)

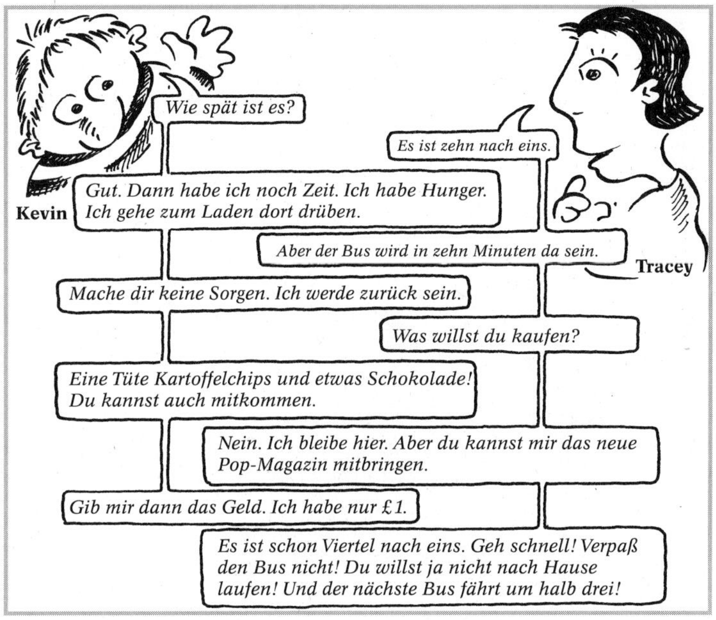

2. *Jetzt könnt ihr die Rollen tauschen. Lest das Gespräch auf englisch ein zweites Mal. Dabei mußt du die deutschen Sätze ins Englische übersetzen. Dein Partner/Deine Partnerin kann dich kontrollieren und umgekehrt.*

3. *Übertrage die deutschen Sätze nun schriftlich ins Englische. Vergleiche zum Schluß mit dem Blatt deines Partners/deiner Partnerin.*

[4.] *Ihr könnt das Gespräch auswendig lernen und vor der Klasse spielen.*

70

WORD GAMES

1. Mrs Baker has a lot of hobbies, but what is her favourite hobby?
First put the words in the right places in the puzzle. Then put the letters in the marked squares in the right order and answer the question.
(Setze die Wörter zuerst richtig in das Puzzle ein. Dann setze die Buchstaben aus den markierten Feldern in die richtige Reihenfolge, um die Frage zu beantworten.)

TENNIS – FOOTBALL – RIDING – DANCING – SWIMMING – PHOTOS – GARDENING

Mrs Baker's favourite hobby is F I S H I N G

2. Joan is in a sports club. What does she play?

3. Mike is in another sports club. What does he play?

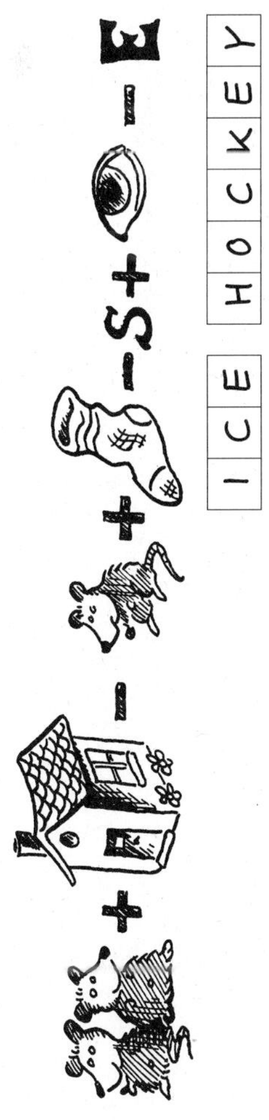

68

LETTER SQUARE

s	t	g	i	v	e	n	u	n	p	q	i	m	b	l
g	v	w	s	b	a	e	r	z	x	e	i	r	r	m
b	e	e	n	n	v	r	m	a	d	e	f	n	o	p
k	l	m	u	o	n	t	q	a	n	e	i	t	u	o
b	r	s	l	e	f	t	p	s	e	e	n	w	g	n
r	p	e	c	p	v	v	h	v	d	t	u	o	h	w
o	o	s	s	w	r	e	z	r	e	a	d	j	t	g
k	n	t	r	r	o	h	e	k	a	q	k	d	n	x
e	d	g	h	i	m	e	g	y	f	a	l	l	e	n
n	w	e	i	t	d	j	o	w	q	m	h	e	l	p
c	s	a	p	t	n	e	n	h	f	p	r	c	j	u
d	w	t	v	e	c	o	e	i	o	c	v	r	y	t
g	l	e	o	n	m	f	r	b	o	u	g	h	t	k
l	d	n	i	n	v	t	r	k	e	a	m	i	x	z
i	k	p	t	a	k	e	n	x	o	l	t	v	m	a

1. Can you find the 15 past participles (3rd forms) of verbs hidden in this letter square? The first one is done for you.
(Kannst du die 15 Verben in der Perfektform (3. Form) finden, die in diesem Wortkasten versteckt sind?)

2. Write the past participles down in the right places in the table below, then complete the table. Look in your English book if you are not sure.
(Trage die Perfektformen aus dem Wortkasten an der richtigen Stelle in die Tabelle unten ein. Dann schreibe die fehlenden Infinitive, *beziehungsweise* Past tense *Formen in die Tabelle. Schau in deinem Englischbuch nach, wenn du dir nicht sicher bist.)*

Infinitive (1st form)	**Past tense** (2nd form)	**Past participle** (3rd form)
give	*gave*	*given*
be / is	was/were	been
bring	brought	brought
make	made	made
break	broke	broken
eat	ate	eaten
leave	left	left
read	read	read
write	wrote	written
see	saw	seen
go	went	gone
take	took	taken
fall	fell	fallen
buy	bought	bought
put	put	put

Betty's party

Betty's parents have gone away for the weekend. Last night Betty and her friends had a big party in the living room.

Now they are in a hurry to clean up the mess. It's 11 o'clock.

1. Now it's 12 o'clock. What have Betty and her friends just done?

has/have just + 3rd form

Tom has just done the washing up. Chris and Jane have just taken the empty bottles to the container. Mary has just put away the glasses. Fiona has just cleaned the floor in the kitchen. Sandra has just bought some new flowers for the table. Bob and Sally have just repaired the bookshelf. Dave and Eric have just washed the table-cloth. Linda has just cleaned the carpet in the living room. Alan has just repaired the record player. Martin and Betty have just made a cake for her Mum and Dad.

2. On Monday Betty tells her friends at school who did what in the house.

past tense! 2nd form!

Tom did the washing up. Chris and Jane took the empty bottles to the container. Mary put away the glasses. Fiona cleaned the floor in the kitchen. Sandra bought some new flowers for the table. Bob and Sally repaired the bookshelf. Dave and Eric washed the table-cloth. Linda cleaned the carpet in the living room. Alan repaired the record player. Martin and I made a cake for my Mum and Dad.

A At the Doctor's

You are on holiday in England. One day you are ill so you go to the doctor's.

1. Work with a partner. You take part A, your partner takes part B. You are Thomas. *(Lies das Gespräch mit einem Partner/einer Partnerin. Du bist Thomas.)*

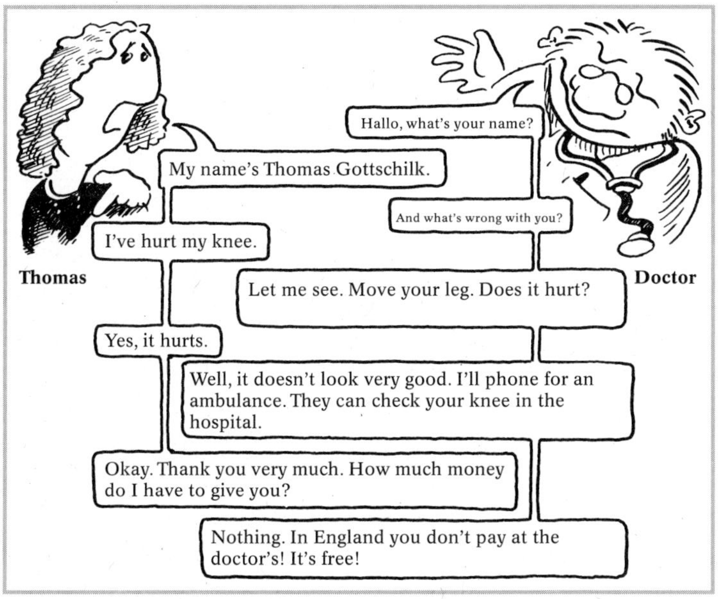

2. *Jetzt könnt ihr die Rollen tauschen. Lest das Gespräch auf englisch ein zweites Mal. Dabei mußt du die deutschen Sätze ins Englische übersetzen. Dein Partner/ Deine Partnerin kann dich kontrollieren und umgekehrt.*

3. *Übertrage die deutschen Sätze nun schriftlich ins Englische. Vergleiche zum Schluß mit dem Blatt deines Partners/deiner Partnerin.*

[4.] *Ihr könnt das Gespräch auswendig lernen und vor der Klasse spielen.*

CUT HERE

B At the Doctor's

Your friend is on holiday in England. One day he is ill so he goes to the doctor's.

1. Work with a partner. You take part B, your partner takes part A. You are the doctor. *(Lies das Gespräch mit einem Partner/einer Partnerin. Du bist der Arzt.)*

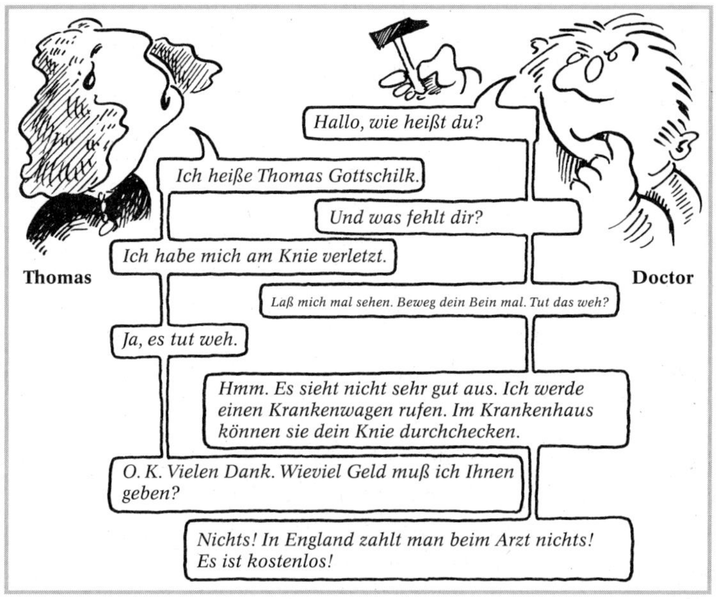

2. *Jetzt könnt ihr die Rollen tauschen. Lest das Gespräch auf englisch ein zweites Mal. Dabei mußt du die deutschen Sätze ins Englische übersetzen. Dein Partner/ Deine Partnerin kann dich kontrollieren und umgekehrt.*

3. *Übertrage die deutschen Sätze nun schriftlich ins Englische. Vergleiche zum Schluß mit dem Blatt deines Partners/deiner Partnerin.*

[4.] *Ihr könnt das Gespräch auswendig lernen und vor der Klasse spielen.*

74

Parts of the body

73

1. Can you find the 13 parts of the body in this word snake?

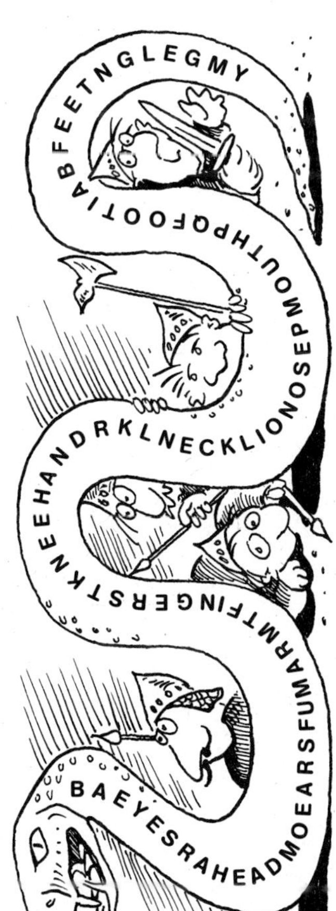

eyes, head, ears, arm, fingers, knee, hand, neck, nose, mouth, foot, feet, leg

2. Man or monster? Write down the English words:

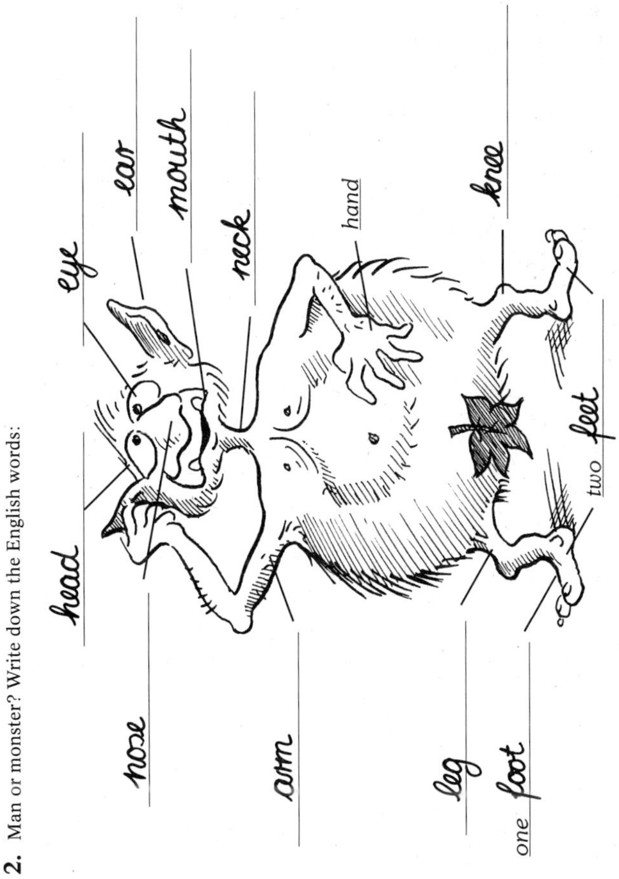

3. Odd man out. *(Welches Wort paßt nicht zu den anderen?)*

a) ears, mouth, eyes, nose, ~~leg~~

b) arm, ~~nose~~, hand, finger

c) knee, feet, ~~ears~~, leg

d) head, ears, eyes, nose, ~~knee~~

[4.] Draw a monster and label it! *(Zeichne selber ein Monster und beschrifte die Körperteile.)*

There was a hurricane in Greentown.
Everything got mixed up.

A HURRICANE

Now the hurricane has gone. Can you write down the things where they belong?
(Kannst du die Namen der Dinge dort eintragen, wo sie hingehören?)

Pets	Food
fish	biscuits
cats	sandwiches
guinea pig	toast
dogs	cakes
rabbit	hamburger
hamsters	beans
budgie	salad
	jam tarts

Things you use to eat and drink	Things you see in the street	Tools
plates	*van*	nails
cups	police car	screws
spoons	motor-bike	screwdriver
knives	bus	plug
saucer	ambulance	hammer
forks	cars	electric saw
teaspoon	bike	drill
tea pot	bridge	

FOLD HERE

Here are the names of the things:

BISCUITSFISHPOLICECARPLATESNAILSCATSSANDWICHESMOTOR-BIKESCREWS
GUINEAPIGTOASTCUPSSCREWDRIVERSPOONSDOGSCAKESPLUGKNIVESBUS
HAMMERSAUCERAMBULANCERABBITFORKSHAMBURGERCARSHAMSTERSBIKE
TEASPOONELECTRICSAWBRIDGEBEANSDRILLSALADTEAPOTBUDGIEJAMTARTS

HOLIDAY POSTCARDS

1. Which text belongs to which postcard?
(Welcher Text gehört mit welcher Postkarte zusammen?)

a = 2 b = 3 c = 1

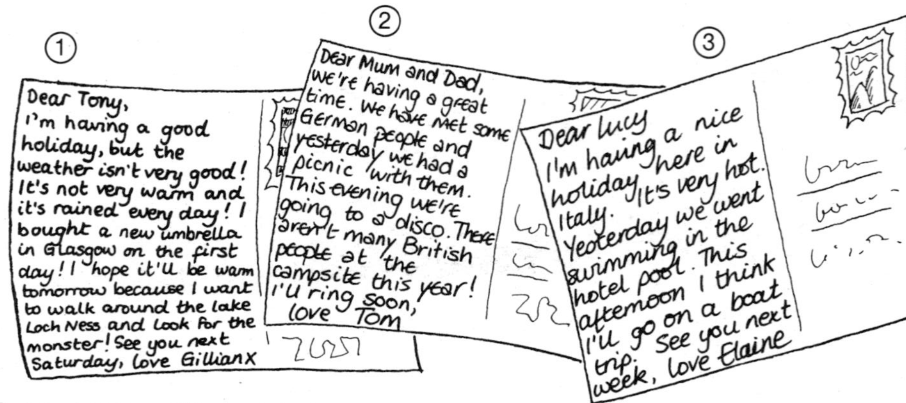

2. Who is it? Tom, Gillian or Elaine?

Elaine Tom Gillian